SOUND INNOVATIONS

for CONCERT BAND

A Revolutionary Method for Beginning Musicians

Robert **SHELDON** | Peter **BOONSHAFT** | Dave **BLACK** | Bob **PHILLIPS**

Congratulations on deciding to be a member of the band!

This book is here to help you get started on a very exciting time in your life. The audio recordings and DVD will help you practice and develop new skills. When you complete the book, you'll be well prepared to play many types and styles of music. Playing in the band will bring you many years of incredible experiences.

Maybe you'll make music an important part of your life by attending concerts, playing in a community band and supporting the arts. Maybe you'll pursue a career in music as a performer, teacher, composer, sound engineer or conductor. Whatever you choose, we wish you the best of luck in becoming a part of the wonderful world of music!

Practice *Sound Innovations* with SmartMusic® Interactive Software

Transform the way you practice. Instead of practicing alone, you play with background accompaniment and hear how your part fits within the whole. *And*, you get instant feedback. You see which notes you've played right or wrong and hear a recording of your performance.

Try SmartMusic today! Get the first 100 lines of music—free—by downloading SmartMusic at **www.smartmusic.com** to get started. Use code SIBAND when prompted during the activation process.

The MP3 CD includes recorded accompaniments for every line of music in your *Sound Innovations* book. These instrument-specific recordings can be played with the included SI Player, easily uploaded to your MP3 player or transferred to your computer. Additionally, many CD and DVD players are equipped to play MP3s directly from the disc. To play an accompaniment, simply choose the file that corresponds to the line of music in the book. Each line has been numbered and named for easy reference.

Also included on the MP3 CD is the SI Player *with* Tempo Change Technology. The SI Player features the ability to change the speed of the recordings without changing pitch—slow the tempo down for practice or speed it up to performance tempo! Use this program to easily play the included MP3 files or any audio file on your computer.

Instrument photos courtesy of Yamaha Corporation of America Band & Orchestral Division
CD Recorded and Mixed at The Lodge Recording Studios, Indianapolis, IN
Electric Bass Performance on CD by: Steve Dokken
Accompaniments Written and Recorded by: Derek Richard
Ensembles Performed by: American Symphonic Winds, Anthony Maiello, Conductor
Production Company: Specialized Personnel Locators
Engineer: Kendall S. Thomsen
DVD Filming and Production: David Darling, Grand Haven, MI
Electric Bass Artist on DVD: Jason Shea

ISBN-10: 0-7390-6737-0
ISBN-13: 978-0-7390-6737-6

Ready? Set? Play! 📀
Sound advice for getting started on your instrument

1. YOUR INSTRUMENT– PARTS OF THE ELECTRIC BASS

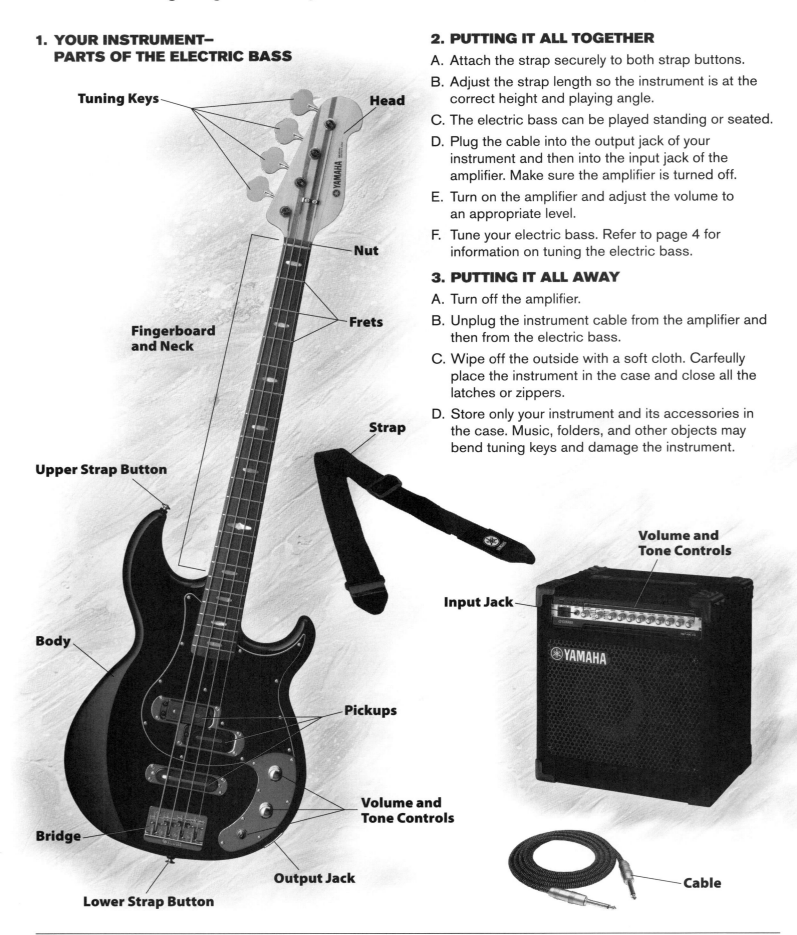

Tuning Keys

Head

Nut

Fingerboard and Neck

Frets

Upper Strap Button

Strap

Body

Pickups

Bridge

Volume and Tone Controls

Output Jack

Lower Strap Button

Input Jack

Volume and Tone Controls

YAMAHA

Cable

2. PUTTING IT ALL TOGETHER

A. Attach the strap securely to both strap buttons.

B. Adjust the strap length so the instrument is at the correct height and playing angle.

C. The electric bass can be played standing or seated.

D. Plug the cable into the output jack of your instrument and then into the input jack of the amplifier. Make sure the amplifier is turned off.

E. Turn on the amplifier and adjust the volume to an appropriate level.

F. Tune your electric bass. Refer to page 4 for information on tuning the electric bass.

3. PUTTING IT ALL AWAY

A. Turn off the amplifier.

B. Unplug the instrument cable from the amplifier and then from the electric bass.

C. Wipe off the outside with a soft cloth. Carfeully place the instrument in the case and close all the latches or zippers.

D. Store only your instrument and its accessories in the case. Music, folders, and other objects may bend tuning keys and damage the instrument.

Please refer to the Sound Innovations *DVD for detailed instructions and demonstrations of assembly, dissassembly and maintenance of your instrument. Whenever you see this icon* 📀*, refer to your DVD for further demonstrations.*

First Sounds 🔵DVD

POSTURE AND PLAYING POSITION

A. Sitting: Sit on the front edge of the chair with feet flat on the floor.

Standing: Stand with feet shoulder width apart.

B. Your left thumb and fingers should form a reverse "C."

C. The pads of your left fingers come directly down on the strings with your left thumb behind the neck.

D. When depressing strings, each finger on your left hand is placed as close as possible behind the fret being played to get the best sound.

E. Place your right thumb on the corner of the fingerboard, corner of the pickup, or on the E string.

F. Your right index and middle fingers alternate pulling through the string and resting on the next string.

G. Keep your fingers of both hands relaxed and naturally curved as if holding a ball.

PLAYING YOUR FIRST SOUNDS

A. Without touching any of the strings with your left hand, locate the D string (2nd smallest).

B. With your right index finger, pull through the D string so that your finger comes to rest on the A string.

C. With your right middle finger, repeat the process.

D. Play several Ds in a row alternating fingers. Use your index and middle fingers.

DAMPENING THE TONE

A. You can stop the tone between notes by touching the vibrating string with your fingers from either hand.

B. When playing fretted notes, you can dampen the tone by slightly lifting the finger pressing down on the string.

EQUIPMENT NEEDS

A. Keep a soft cloth in your case for maintaining your instrument.

B. Store your cable away carefully.

LEARNING FINGER NUMBERS

A. Turn your left hand so the palm is toward your face.

B. Tap your thumb against your 1st finger, your 2nd finger, your 3rd finger, and your 4th finger.

Sound Notation

Music has its own language and symbols that are recognized worldwide.

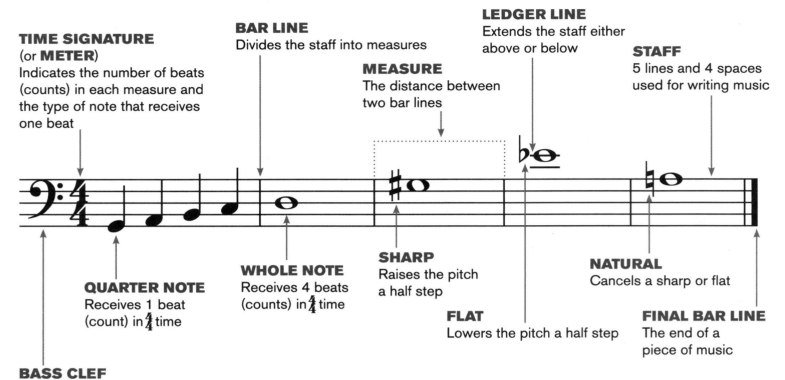

TIME SIGNATURE
(or **METER**)
Indicates the number of beats
(counts) in each measure and
the type of note that receives
one beat

BAR LINE
Divides the staff into measures

MEASURE
The distance between
two bar lines

LEDGER LINE
Extends the staff either
above or below

STAFF
5 lines and 4 spaces
used for writing music

QUARTER NOTE
Receives 1 beat
(count) in 4/4 time

WHOLE NOTE
Receives 4 beats
(counts) in 4/4 time

SHARP
Raises the pitch
a half step

NATURAL
Cancels a sharp or flat

FLAT
Lowers the pitch a half step

FINAL BAR LINE
The end of a
piece of music

BASS CLEF
Also called F clef (the 4th line of the staff is F
and the clef is drawn by starting on the F Line)
and includes a dot above and below the F line

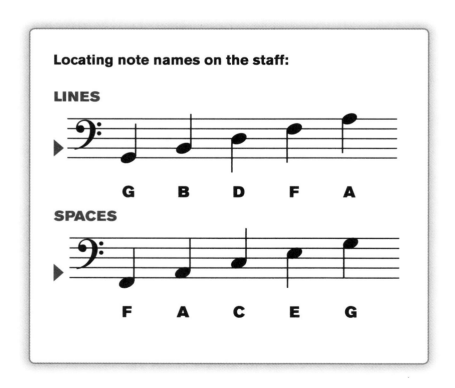

Locating note names on the staff:

LINES

G B D F A

SPACES

F A C E G

HOW TO PRACTICE

As you play through this book, some parts will
be very easy while others may require more time
to play well. Practicing your instrument every
day will help you achieve excellence. Carefully
play each exercise until you can perform it
comfortably three times in succession.

▶ Practice in a quiet place where you
can concentrate.

▶ Schedule a regular practice time every day.

▶ Use a straight back chair and a music stand
to assist you in maintaining good posture.

▶ Start each practice session by checking your
posture and hand positions.

▶ Focus on the music that is most difficult to
play, then move on to that which is easier
and more fun.

▶ Use your recordings to help you play in tune
and in time. Refer to your DVD as marked.

Track 1—Tuning Track
Listen to the open strings and adjust your tuning
keys. Your teacher will show you how to use an
electronic tuner.

Level 1: Sound Beginnings

The **BASS CLEF** (F Clef) identifies the location of notes on the staff. The two dots of the bass clef are above and below the F on the staff. F is on the 4th line.

A **TIME SIGNATURE** or **METER** indicates the number of beats (counts) in each measure and the kind of note that receives one beat.

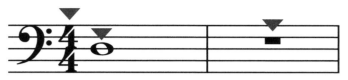

TIME is a meter in which there are 4 beats per measure and the quarter note receives 1 beat.

Count: **1+2+3+4+** **1+2+3+4+**
(+ = "and")

WHOLE NOTES receive 4 beats (counts) in 4/4 time.

WHOLE RESTS indicate a full measure of silence.

OUR FIRST NOTE *Introducing the new note, D.*

1+2+3+4+ 1+2+3+4+

OUR SECOND NOTE *Introducing the new note, C.*

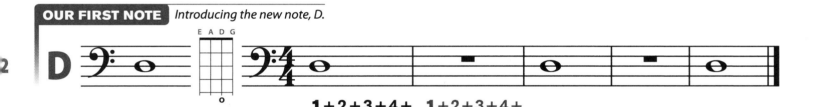

TWO-NOTE TANGO—*Practice going from one note to the other.*

OUR THIRD NOTE *Introducing the new note, B♭.*

THREE-NOTE COMBO—*Practice playing all three notes.*

6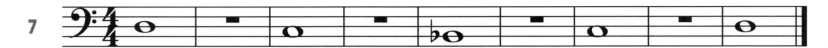

THIRD TIME'S THE CHARM—*Additional practice on these three notes.*

7

A **SOLO** is when one person is performing alone or with accompaniment.

MATCH THE PITCH—*Play the solo part as the rest of the band answers with the same note. Take turns with other band members.*

8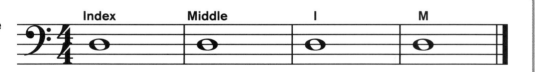

Alternate the index and middle fingers of the right hand when playing consecutive notes.

A BREATH OF FRESH AIR—*Name each note before you play.*

9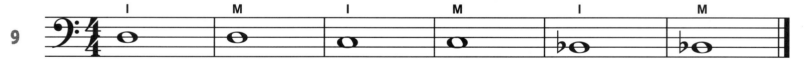

BREATHING EASY—*Sing the notes, then play.*

10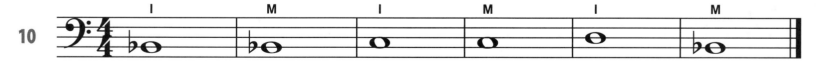

THREE-ZY DOES IT!—*Practice playing three different notes in a row.*

11

HALF NOTES receive two beats (counts) in 4/4 time.

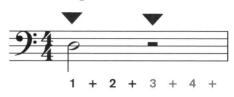

1 + 2 + 3 + 4 +

HALF RESTS receive two beats (counts) of silence and look similar to whole rests. Since half rests only contain two beats, they are "light" and therefore float above the line. Because most whole rests contain an entire measure of beats, they are "heavier" and therefore sink below the line.

The **REPEAT SIGN** tells you to go back to the beginning and play the piece again.

HALF THE TIME—*Introducing half notes and half rests. Repeat as indicated. Clap the rhythm as you count the beats, then sing the piece before you play.*

1 + 2 + 3 + 4 +   1 + 2 + 3 + 4 +

MIX IT UP—*Play each group of half notes using alternating right-hand fingers.*

A **DUET** is a composition for two performers. When both parts are played together, you will sometimes hear two different notes played at the same time which creates **HARMONY**.

DUET? DO IT!—*Introducing our first duet.*

NAME THE NOTES—*Write the name of each note in the space provided, then sing the notes before you play.*

____   ____   ____   ____   ____   ____

QUARTER NOTES receive one beat (count) in $\frac{4}{4}$ time.
QUARTER RESTS receive one beat (count) of silence.

1 + 2 + 3 + 4 +   1 + 2 + 3 + 4 +

QUARTER NOTES—*Introducing quarter notes and quarter rests. Count, clap and sing before you play.*

16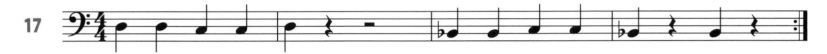

1 + 2 + 3 + 4 +   1 + 2 + 3 + 4 +

QUARTERLY REPORT—*Name each note before you play.*

17

A **PHRASE** is a musical idea.

HOT CROSS BUNS—*Play the phrase, not just the notes!*

English Folk Song

18

 **OUR FOURTH NOTE** *Introducing the new note, E♭.*

19

SCALING THE WALL—*Practice using your newest note.*

20

OUR FIFTH NOTE *Introducing the new note, F.*

21

SCALING NEW HEIGHTS—*Practice using another new note.*

22

MERRILY WE ROLL ALONG—*Hold your left-hand first finger down through the entire last bar.*

Traditional

AU CLAIRE DE LA LUNE—*Play smoothly.*

French Folk Song

COMMON TIME is another name for the 4/4 time signature and is indicated with this symbol:

A **FERMATA** tells you to hold a note or rest longer than its normal duration.

A **COMPOSER** is a person who writes music. Look for the composer's name on the upper right corner of the music.

Who wrote the music to *Jingle Bells*?

JINGLE BELLS—*Play this piece in common time and notice the fermata at the end. Count, clap and sing before you play.*

James Lord Pierpont

1 + 2 + 3 + 4 +

GO TELL AUNT RHODY—*More practice in common time with a fermata.*

American Folk Song

LIGHTLY ROW—*Play this duet in common time. Switch parts on the repeat.*

Traditional

TUTTI tells you that everyone plays together.

GOOD KING WENCESLAS—*The soloist and full band take turns playing.*

Traditional English Carol

solo   tutti   solo   tutti

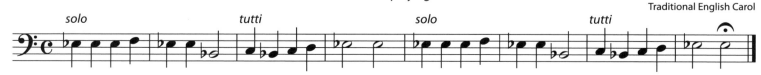

> A **ROUND** is a type of music in which players start the piece at different times, creating interesting harmonies and accompaniments.

SWEETLY SINGS THE DONKEY (round)—*Play this round by having players or groups start every four measures. This piece continues on the next staff, which does not need to show the meter.*

American Folk Song

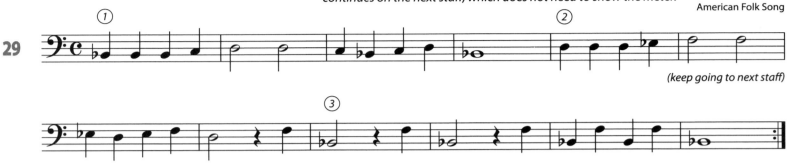

(keep going to next staff)

FERMATAS 'R US—*Your teacher will indicate how long to hold each fermata.*

DREYDL, DREYDL—*Here is a holiday song that uses all the notes you have learned.*

Traditional Hanukkah Song

> A **TIE** is a curved line that connects two or more notes of the same pitch. The tied notes are played as one longer note with the combined value of both notes.
>
>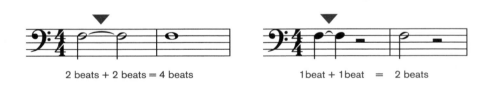
>
> 2 beats + 2 beats = 4 beats   1 beat + 1 beat = 2 beats
>
> ---
>
> A **WARM-UP** is an important part of your daily preparation. Focus on producing a beautiful sound.   A **CHORALE** is a harmonized melody played slowly. Many bands play chorales as part of their warm-up.

WARM-UP CHORALE—*Play with a beautiful sustained tone. Listen for the harmony!*

TIE AND TIE AGAIN—*Play the tied notes full value. This piece can be played as a duet along with the Warm-Up Chorale.*

▶ Complete the **SOUND CHECK** near the end of your book.

Level 2: Sound Fundamentals

OUR SIXTH NOTE *Introducing the new note, G.*

34

TWINKLING STARS—*Play this familiar melody using your new note.*

Adapted by Wolfgang Amadeus Mozart

35

(keep going to next staff)

36 JOLLY OLD ST. NICK—*Here is a duet that uses your new note.*

Traditional Carol

A

B

New Time Signature (Meter) 2/4 TIME

2 = Two beats (counts) per measure.
4 = A quarter note receives one beat (count).

RHYTHMS IN 2/4—*Clap the rhythm while counting the beats aloud.*

1 + 2 + 1 + 2 + 1 + 2 + 1 + 2 +

TWO-FOUR OUT THE DOOR—*This exercise has two beats per measure. Count, clap and sing before you play.*

37

1 + 2 + 1 + 2 +

LONDON BRIDGE—*Here's a melody you know in 2/4 time. How many beats does the last note receive?*

English Folk Song

38

TWO-FOUR OLD MAC—*Name each note before you play.*

Traditional

39

TECHNIQUE BUILDER—*Practice slowly at first, then gradually get faster each time you play.*

40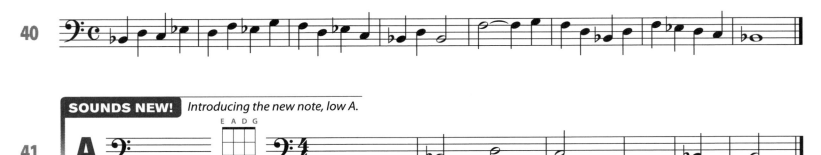

SOUNDS NEW! *Introducing the new note, low A.*

41

MARY ANN—*This calypso (Caribbean dance) tune uses your new note. Notice the long ties over the bar lines. Discuss with your teacher the characteristics of music in different styles. Listen to the recording of this piece and describe this style of music.*

Caribbean Folk Song

42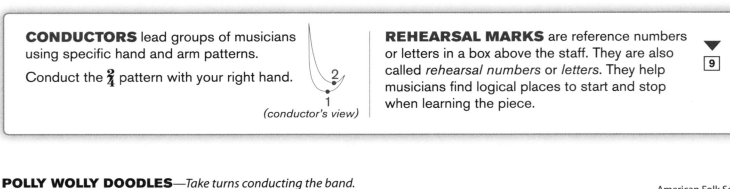

CONDUCTORS lead groups of musicians using specific hand and arm patterns.

Conduct the $\frac{2}{4}$ pattern with your right hand.

2

1

(conductor's view)

REHEARSAL MARKS are reference numbers or letters in a box above the staff. They are also called *rehearsal numbers* or *letters*. They help musicians find logical places to start and stop when learning the piece.

▼

9

POLLY WOLLY DOODLES—*Take turns conducting the band.*

American Folk Song

43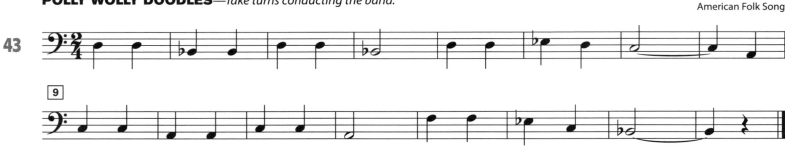

9

44 DUET OF THE CRUSADERS—*This duet uses your new high and low notes.*

German Folk Song

A

B

SHOO-FLY!—*This melody features ties across the bar line.*

American Folk Song

ON THE BRIDGE AT AVIGNON—*Sing the note names, then take turns conducting the band as they play.*

French Folk Song

SOUND THEORY—*Draw a clef, meter (hint: look at the last note), bar lines and a final bar line. Write the names of the notes and number of beats for each note before you play.*

Number of beats: 2   1   1   __ __ __   __ __ __   __ __ __

Note Names: D   E♭   E♭   __ __ __   __ __ __   __ __ __

DIVISI (div.) indicates where two notes appear at the same time. Each note should be played by an equal number of players to achieve a balanced harmony.

UNISON (unis.) indicates where two parts play the same note.

WARM UP—*Play with a beautiful sound and listen to the harmony on the divided notes!*

The **KEY SIGNATURE** appears at the beginning of the staff. It tells you which notes will be played sharp or flat. Different instruments play in different keys. This is in your key of **B-FLAT MAJOR**, with two flats. All B's and E's are flat. Transposing instruments that play in other keys may refer to this as "Concert B-flat Major."

MARCHING MADNESS—*Full band arrangement.*

March tempo

ROCK THIS BAND!—*Full band arrangement.*

Hard rock

50

EIGHTH NOTES each receive a half beat (count) in 4/4 time. Two eighth notes receive one count. Eighth notes often appear in pairs or in groups of four and have a *beam* across the note stems.

1 +   1 + 2 + 3 + 4 +

51   **RHYTHM ROUND-UP**—*Clap the rhythm as you count the beats.*

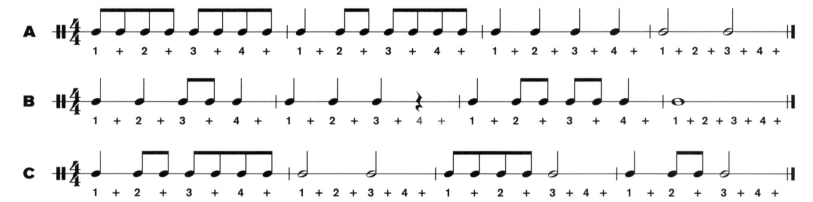

52   **GOTTA HAND IT TO YA! (Clapping Duet)**—*Clap either Part A or B, then switch parts on the repeat.*

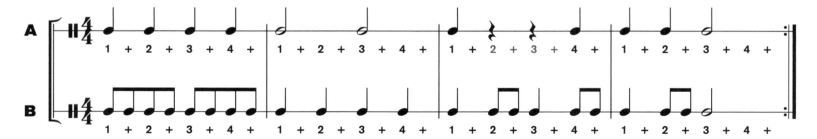

PIECES OF EIGHT—*Count the rhythm first, clap, then play.*

53

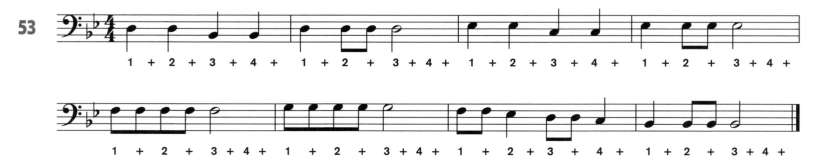

15

DYNAMICS in music refer to the change in volume you create when playing loud or soft. Italian terms are often used in music. The term we use for loud is **FORTE** and is indicated by the letter *f*, and the term we use for quiet (or soft) is **PIANO** and is indicated by the letter *p*. Pull the string with more force to play louder and with less force to play softer.

WHISPER AND SHOUT!—*Play the notes with the dynamics indicated.*

(look ahead to the next line for the dynamic change)

LONG, LONG AGO—*Play this familiar melody with dynamics.*

Thomas Haynes Bayly

(the f carries over to this line)

SKIP TO MY LOU—*More fun with dynamics! Name each note before you play.*

American Folk Song

57 DYNAMIC DUET—*Read the dynamics carefully as they are different in each part. Switch parts on the repeat.*

THIS OLD MAN—*Here is a tune to play just for fun!*

American Folk Song

An **INTERVAL** is the distance between two notes. The interval of an 8th is called an **OCTAVE**. The interval on the same note is a **UNISON**.

SOUNDS NEW! *Introducing the new note, low G.*

59

INTERESTING INTERVALS—*Build your technique. Write the name of each interval in the space provided before you play.*

60

Interval: 2nd   ___   ___   ___   ___   ___   ___   ___   ___   ___   ___   ___

HEY, HO! NOBODY'S HOME—*Practice dynamics.*

English Folk Song

61

DVD A **CRESCENDO** (*cresc.* or ⏜) tells you to gradually play louder. | A **DECRESCENDO** or **DIMINUENDO** (*decresc., dim.* or ⏝) tells you to gradually play softer.

TURN THE VOLUME UP—*Play with more force in your right hand.*

62

TURN THE VOLUME DOWN—*Play with less force in your right hand.*

63

Play smoothly by pulling your index or middle finger all the way to the next lower string.

FRÈRE JACQUES (round)—*Play this familiar melody smoothly, then play it as a round.*

French Folk Song

64

PICKUP NOTES occur before the first complete measure of a phrase. Often the last measure of the piece will be missing the same number of beats as the pickup notes have.

4 +   1 + 2 + 3 + 4 +   1 + 2 + 3 +

A TISKET, A TASKET—*How many beats are in the pickup?*

American Folk Song

65

f
4   +   1 + 2 + 3 + 4 +

p   *cresc.*   *f*

decresc.

1 + 2 + 3 +
(beat 4 is the pickup)

JASMINE FLOWER—*Practice the notes and skills you have learned.*

Chinese Folk Song

66

p   *f*

18

ERIE CANAL—*How many beats are in the pickup? How many beats are missing from the last measure?*

Thomas S. Allen

OH! SUSANNAH—*The pickup contains two eighth notes.*

Stephen Foster

THEME AND VARIATION is a compositional technique in which the composer clearly states a melody (or theme), then changes it by adding contrasting variations.

A **DOUBLE BAR LINE** indicates the end of a section.

THEME AND VARIATIONS ON BLACK SHEEP—*How does Variation I differ from the Theme? How does Variation II differ from the Theme?*

English Folk Song

Theme

Variation I

Variation II

THEME AND VARIATIONS YOUR WAY—*Write your own variation by changing the rhythm and/or notes, then play it!*

Theme: *Hot Cross Buns*

Variation: *Cinnamon Buns*

TEMPO MARKINGS indicate the speed of the music.

LARGO is a slow tempo.
ANDANTE is a moderate walking tempo.
ALLEGRO is a fast tempo.

Conduct the 4/4 pattern with your right hand.

Conduct each piece below at the correct tempo.

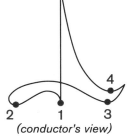

(conductor's view)

Austrian composer **Wolfgang Amadeus Mozart** (1756–1791) was one of the most influential musicians of the Classical period. Though he only lived to the age of 35, he was very prolific and is known for his symphonies, operas, chamber music and piano pieces.

German-born composer **Johannes Brahms** (1833–1897) was one of the leading figures of the Romantic period in music history. Brahms is best known for his four symphonies, two piano concertos and his remarkable choral work *A German Requiem*.

SERENADE—*Full band arrangement.*

Wolfgang Amadeus Mozart

INVADERS!—*Full band arrangement. Remember, in 2/4 time a whole measure rest receives two beats.*

ACADEMIC FESTIVAL OVERTURE—*Full band arrangement.*

Johannes Brahms

STODOLA PUMPA—*Practice good posture.*

Czech Folk Song

More dynamics! **MEZZO FORTE** (*mf*) is medium loud. **MEZZO PIANO** (*mp*) is medium soft.

DYNAMITE DYNAMICS—*Review all four of the dynamics you've learned, along with crescendo and decrescendo.*

Stephen Collins Foster (1826–1864), best known for composing songs such as *Beautiful Dreamer*, *Oh! Susanna* and *Camptown Races*, is often called "the father of American music" and the "first professional songwriter."

MY OLD KENTUCKY HOME—*Solo with piano accompaniment.*

▶ Complete the **SOUND CHECK** near the end of your book.

Level 3: Sound Musicianship

SOUNDS NEW! *Introducing the new note, A♭.*

The new key signature of concert **E-FLAT MAJOR** tells you that all B's, E's and A's are flat.

STYLE MARKINGS are sometimes used instead of tempo markings to help musicians understand the feeling the composer would like the music to convey.

WAY UP HIGH—*Before you play, circle all the notes affected by the key signature. Discuss ways in which you can make this sound "sweet."*

BINGO—*Before playing, discuss ways in which you can make this sound "light." Name the key.*

American Folk Song

1ST AND 2ND ENDINGS: Play the 1st ending the first time through. Repeat the music, but skip over the 1st ending on the repeat and play the 2nd ending instead.

BUFFALO GALS—*Since this is played with spirit, the tempo should be energetic! Watch the 1st and 2nd endings.*

American Traditional

MUSETTE—*Here is a tune to play just for fun!*

Johann Sebastian Bach

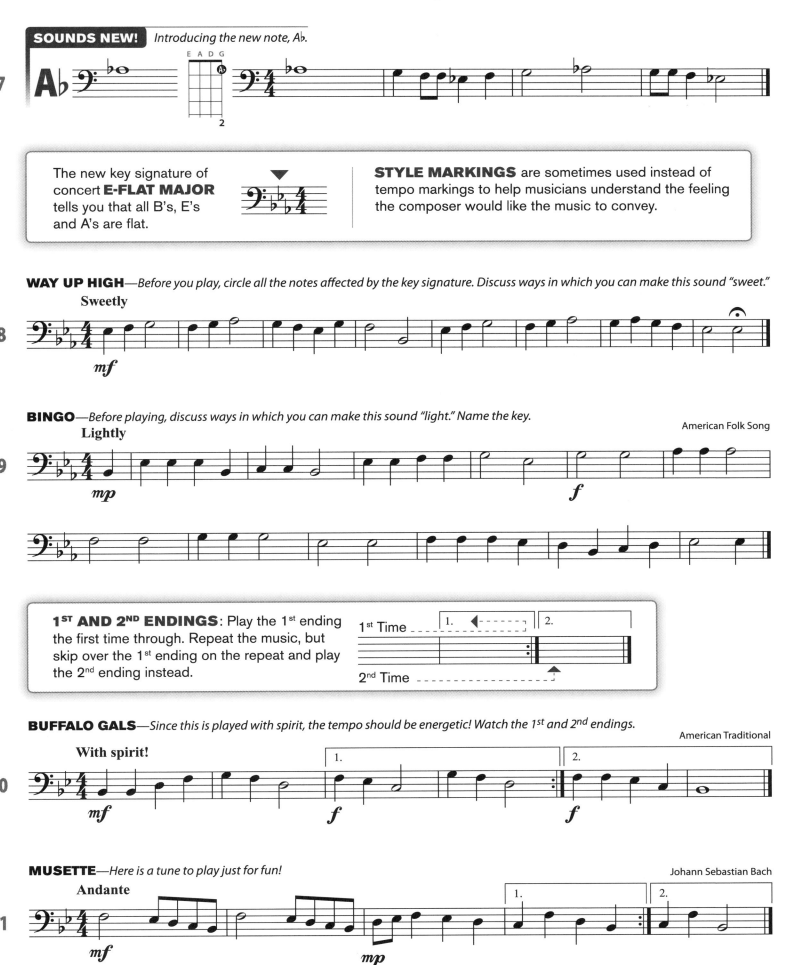

¾ TIME is a meter in which there are 3 beats per measure and the quarter note receives 1 beat.

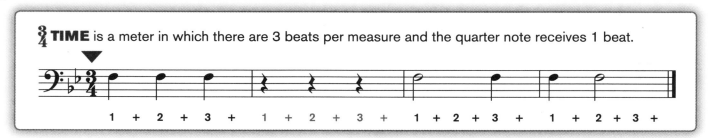

MEXICAN HAT DANCE—*Write the number of each beat you play in the space provided. Count, clap and sing before you play.*
See how well your performance of Mexican Hat Dance captures the style of a dance.

Mexican Folk Song

Allegro

82

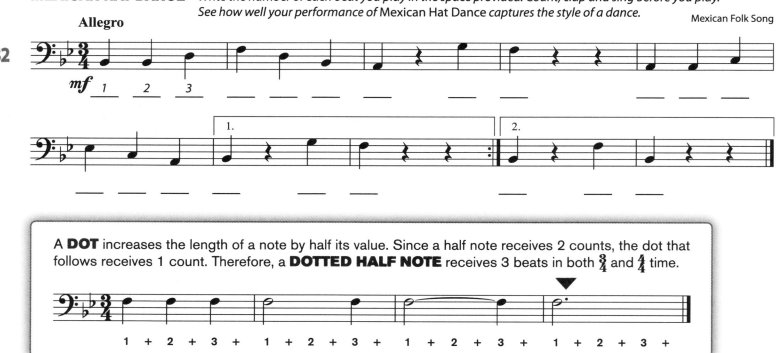

A **DOT** increases the length of a note by half its value. Since a half note receives 2 counts, the dot that follows receives 1 count. Therefore, a **DOTTED HALF NOTE** receives 3 beats in both ¾ and 4/4 time.

BARCAROLLE—*Name the key. Play this in a gentle style. Try memorizing this melody and playing it expressively.*

Jacques Offenbach

Gently

83

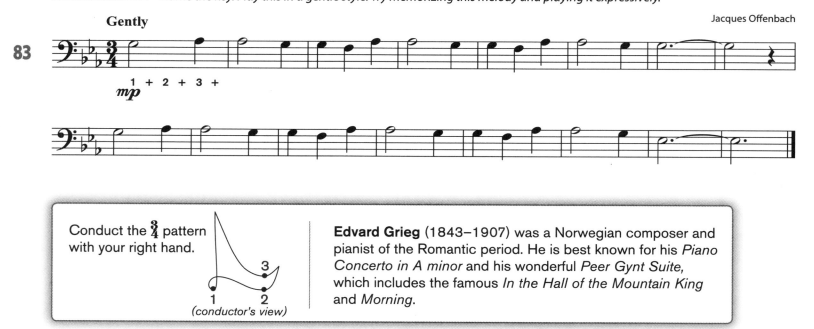

Conduct the ¾ pattern with your right hand.

3

1   2

(conductor's view)

Edvard Grieg (1843–1907) was a Norwegian composer and pianist of the Romantic period. He is best known for his *Piano Concerto in A minor* and his wonderful *Peer Gynt Suite*, which includes the famous *In the Hall of the Mountain King* and *Morning*.

MORNING—*Before you play, sing and conduct the following piece. Moderato is a medium tempo.*

Edvard Grieg

Moderato

84

SOUNDS NEW! *Introducing the new note, low Ab.*

85

An **ACCIDENTAL** is a ♯, ♭, or ♮ sign placed in front of a note to alter its pitch. The effect lasts until the end of the measure. Determine how the key signatures, accidentals and bar lines affect the notes in the following exercise.

TWO-NOTE TREAT

Name the key: ____   *Name the key: ____*   *(the accidental is still in effect)*

86

Name these notes: ____   ____   ____ ____

A **RIGHT-FACING REPEAT** shows where to begin repeating the music.

TRAP-EAZY DOES IT!—*Before you play, think about the repeats.*

Gaston Lyle

Andante

87

mf

1.   2.

SOUNDS NEW! *Introducing the new notes, A and Bb.*

88

TAKE NOTE—*What does* Largo *mean?*

Largo

89

mf

THE CARNIVAL OF VENICE—*Here is another melody with a pickup note and 1st and 2nd endings.*

Italian Folk Song

Moderato

90

f

1.   2.

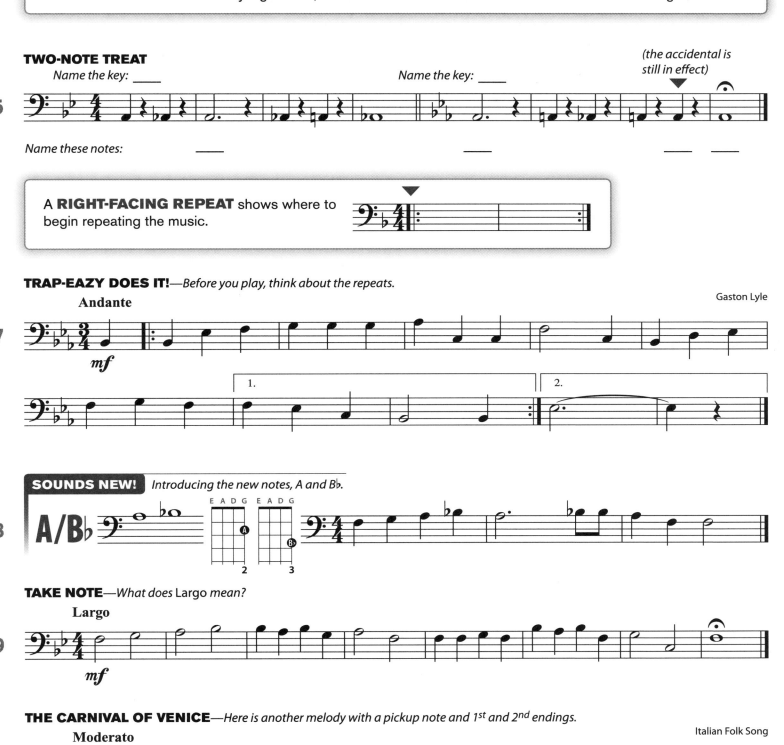

DVD An **ARTICULATION** indicates the way a note should be played. An **ACCENT** is an articulation that tells you the note should be played with a stronger attack. Play an accent by using more force in your right hand.

CHESTER—Chester *was often referred to as the "unofficial anthem" of the American Revolution.*

William Billings

Proudly

91

mf   f

A **ONE-MEASURE REPEAT** means to play the previous measure again.

EIGHTH NOTES and **EIGHTH RESTS** are not always in pairs. They can be single notes and rests. Single eighth notes have a flag on the stem rather than a beam.

MARCHING ALONG—*Circle the accents and the one-measure repeat before you play.*

Moderate march tempo

92

mf   f

---

93 **EXERCISES ON EIGHTHS**—*Demonstrate your understanding of eighth notes and rests by clapping these exercises.*
Switch parts on the repeat.

---

94 **EMPHASIS ON ACCENTS**—*Try both parts of this clapping duet and be sure to clap louder on the accented notes.*
Before you play, circle the single eighth notes and eighth rests in Part B.

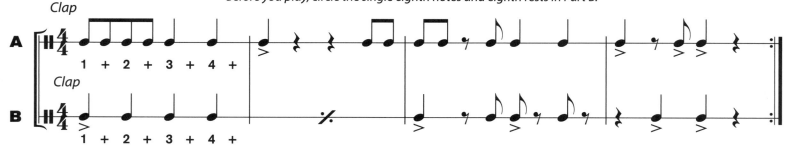

EMPHASIS ON NOTES—*Now play the accents by using more force in your right hand.*

Andante

95

f

DOWN BY THE STATION—*Practice eighth notes and accents.*

Allegro

American Folk Song

96

BROTHER JOHN (round)—*More practice using articulations (accents) and one-measure repeats, then play it as a round.*

Moderato

French Folk Song

97

SOUNDS NEW! *Introducing the new note, E.*

98

The new key signature of concert **F MAJOR** tells you that all B's are flat.

AURA LEE—*How does this new key signature affect the notes you will play?*

Moderato

George R. Poulton

99

SAKURA—*This melody has a right-facing repeat. Before you play, trace your finger over the "roadmap" of the piece.*

Andante

Japanese Folk Song

100

SHE WORE A YELLOW RIBBON—*Here's a tune to play just for fun!*

With spirit!

George A. Norton

101

A quarter note receives 1 beat, and the dot that follows receives ½ a beat, therefore, a **DOTTED QUARTER NOTE** receives 1½ beats and can be subdivided into three eighth notes. (♩. = ♪♪♪)

Count and clap, then play this rhythm. Notice that the quarter note tied to the eighth sounds the same as the dotted quarter note.

A WHOLE LOTTA TIES—*Feel the pulse of the beat on the tied eighth note.*

Moderato

102

A WHOLE LOTTA DOTS—*Feel the pulse of the beat on the dot.*

Moderato

103

D.C. AL FINE indicates to repeat from the beginning and play to the **FINE** (the end).

Antonín Leopold Dvořák (1841–1904) was a Czech composer of the Romantic period best known for drawing inspiration from folk music and for his remarkable *New World Symphony* and *Slavonic Dances*.

THEME FROM THE "NEW WORLD SYMPHONY"—*Play the D.C., then end at the Fine.*

Antonín Dvořák

104

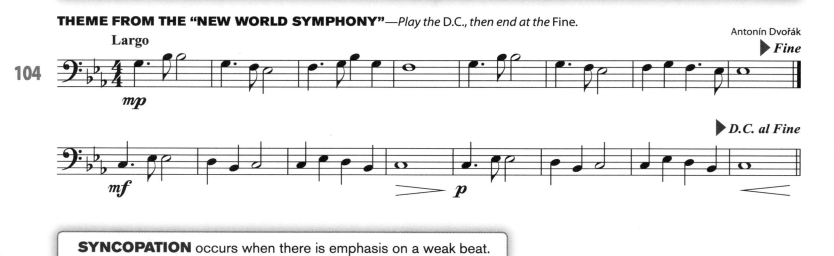

SYNCOPATION occurs when there is emphasis on a weak beat.

JOY TO THE WORLD—*Full band arrangement.*

Christmas Carol

105

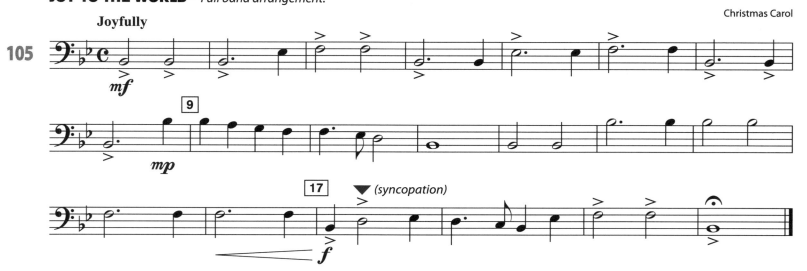

COURTESY ACCIDENTALS help remind you of the key signature. They usually occur after another accidental or a recent key change. These special accidentals are enclosed in parentheses.

ACCIDENTAL ENCOUNTERS—*Before you play, name all the notes.*

(notice the key signature change)

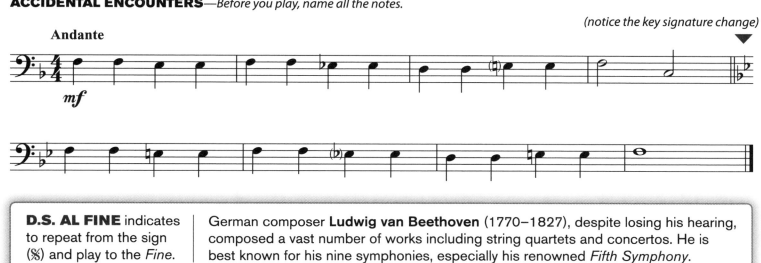

D.S. AL FINE indicates to repeat from the sign (𝄋) and play to the *Fine*.

German composer **Ludwig van Beethoven** (1770–1827), despite losing his hearing, composed a vast number of works including string quartets and concertos. He is best known for his nine symphonies, especially his renowned *Fifth Symphony*.

ODE TO JOY—Maestoso *means to play majestically. Circle the "sign" then clap, count and sing before you play.*

Ludwig van Beethoven

A **MULTIPLE-MEASURE REST** tells you to rest for more than one full measure. The number above the staff tells you how many measures you rest.

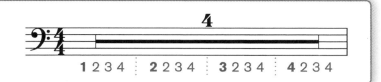

AULD LANG SYNE—*Full band arrangement. Circle the multiple-measure rest before you play.*

Scottish Folk Song

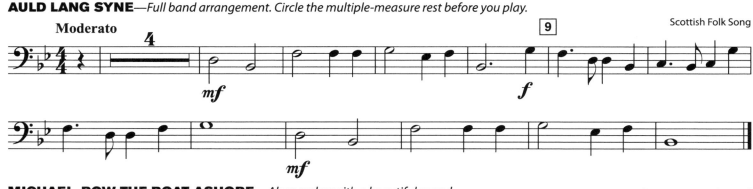

MICHAEL, ROW THE BOAT ASHORE—*Always play with a beautiful sound.*

African-American Spiritual

▶ Complete the **SOUND CHECK** near the end of your book.

Level 4: Sound Development

A **SCALE** is a series of notes that ascend or descend stepwise (consecutive notes) within a key. The lowest and the highest notes of the scale are always the same letter name and are an octave apart.

A **WALTZ** is a popular dance in ¾ time.

CONCERT B♭ MAJOR SCALE—*Memorize this scale!*

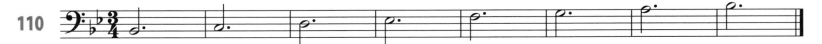

THREE-FOUR, PHRASE SOME MORE—*This melody starts with a phrase that sounds as if it asks a question, followed by a phrase that sounds as if it provides the answer. Play this as a duet with the Concert B♭ scale.*

Waltz tempo

DOWN THE ROAD—*Play with a steady amount of force in your right hand.*

SUO GAN—*Play this melody in the style of a lullaby.*

Moderato

Welsh Folk Song

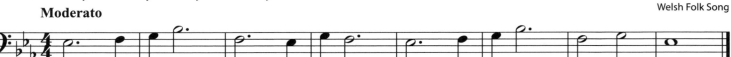

LEGATO (–) is an articulation or style of playing that is smooth and connected. It is indicated by a line. Let the string ring through the entire note.

STACCATO (·) is an articulation or style of playing that is light and separated. It is indicated with a dot. Stop the string from ringing through the entire note by dampening the string.

ARTICULATION STATION—*Play the notes with the indicated articulation.* **DVD**

OVERTURE TO "WILLIAM TELL"—*Here is a familiar tune that uses legato and staccato.*

Allegro

Gioacchino Rossini

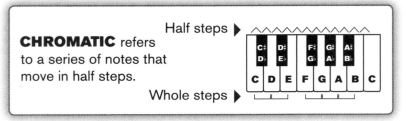

CHROMATIC refers to a series of notes that move in half steps.

Half steps ▶

Whole steps ▶

CHROMATIC MARCH—Alla marcia *instructs us to play in the style of a march.*

Alla marcia

122

123 **JAZZ DOO-ETTE**—*Play this piece in the style of the "jazz big bands" popular in the 1930s and 1940s. Name the key.*

Swing

A

B

ON YOUR OWN!—*Play the first four measures, then write the last four measures yourself! Now, play the entire piece.*

Andante

124

MUSIC MY WAY! Write your own composition:
- Write in the clef, meter, key signature, tempo and style you choose.
- Place the notes and rhythms that you already know on the staff in any order you like and add a final bar line.
- Add articulations (staccato, legato, accents, slurs) and dynamics (*p*, *mp*, *mf*, *f*, *cresc.*, *decresc.*).
- Give the piece a title, and be sure to add **YOUR NAME** as the composer.
- Now play the piece for your friends and family!

Title: _____   Composed by _____

CAN-CAN—*Vivo means lively and spirited!*

Jacques Offenbach

Vivo

125

VOLGA BOAT SONG—Pesante *means to play in a heavy style. Memorize this piece and play in an expressive manner.*

Pesante

Russian Folk Song

With your teacher, develop a list of rules for good concert etiquette. Some things to include might be to listen quietly and to show your appreciation by applauding at the end of the piece. Take turns performing *All Through the Night* while others in your class practice good concert etiquette.

ALL THROUGH THE NIGHT—*Name the key.*

Andante

Welsh Folk Song

ARIRANG—*Name the key. Discuss with your teacher the characteristics of music from different cultures. Listen to the recording of this piece and describe those characteristics.*

Gently

Korean Folk Song

MINUET—*A minuet is a French country dance.*

Stately

Johann Sebastian Bach

Take turns performing *Sailor's Chantey* while other members of the class evaluate the performance using criteria developed with your teacher. Consider rhythm, intonation, tone, dynamics, phrasing and expression.

SAILOR'S CHANTEY—*Name the key.*

Andante

Sea Chantey

THEME FROM SWAN LAKE—*Always play with expression.*

Mournfully

Pyotr Il'yich Tchaikovsky

Most of the music we hear is either in a **MAJOR** key or a **MINOR** key. The sound of these keys is created by the arrangement of half steps and whole steps. The mood of a major key is often cheerful or heroic, while a minor key may be sad or solemn.

MAJOR MACARONI (YANKEE DOODLE)—*This is in a major key. How does this make you feel?*

American Traditional

MINOR MACARONI—*This is in a minor key. How does this make you feel? How is it different from Major Macaroni?*

ALOUETTE—*Is this in a major or minor key?*

French-Canadian Folk Song

HATIKVAH—*Does this sound like a major or minor key?*

Israeli National Anthem

MARCH SLAV—*Is this in a major or minor key?*

Pyotr Il'yich Tchaikovsky

▶ Complete the **SOUND CHECK** near the end of your book.

Level 5: Sound Techniques

An **INTERLUDE** is a short musical piece. The following *Imperative Interludes* will help you practice crossing strings when playing large intervals.

RANGE ROVER 1

IMPERATIVE INTERLUDE 1

RANGE ROVER 2

IMPERATIVE INTERLUDE 2

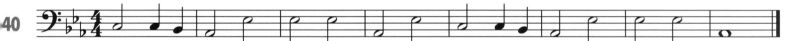

RANGE ROVER 3

IMPERATIVE INTERLUDE 3

HIGH FLYING—*Here's a tune to play just for fun!*

Andante

RANGE ROVER 4

144

IMPERATIVE INTERLUDE 4

145

RANGE ROVER 5

146

IMPERATIVE INTERLUDE 5

147

RANGE ROVER 6

148

IMPERATIVE INTERLUDE 6

149

DRINK TO ME ONLY WITH THINE EYES—*Practice playing smoothly with this familiar tune.*

Moderato

Traditional English Song

150

mf

IT'S RAINING, IT'S POURING—*Play this familiar melody with a beautiful sound.*

English Folk Song

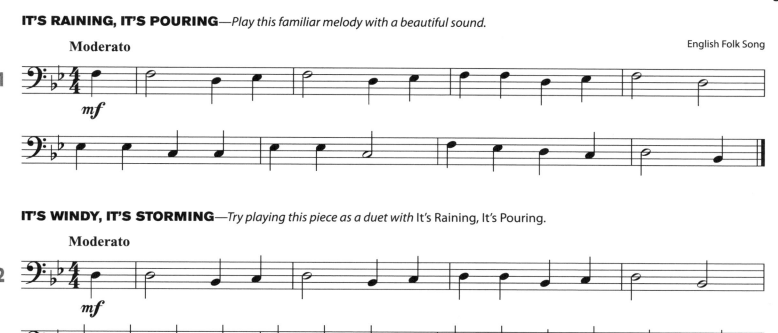

IT'S WINDY, IT'S STORMING—*Try playing this piece as a duet with* It's Raining, It's Pouring.

RANGE RIDER

CRAZY FINGERS

RANGE ROVER 7

IMPERATIVE INTERLUDE 7

SWORD DANCE—*Here's a tune to play just for fun!*

Traditional

BREAK UP—*Play the phrase, not just the notes.*

NEW NOTE! *Introducing the new note, high C.*

158

BREAK DOWN—*Play with a steady amount of force in your right hand.*

159

DOWN AND OUT—*Play with a full sound.*

Moderato

160

UP AND OVER—*Demonstrate good posture.*

Moderato

161

THE CONCERT B♭ MAJOR SCALE—*Memorize the following ascending and descending scale.*

162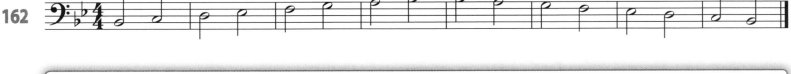

An **ARPEGGIO** is the 1st, 3rd, 5th and 8th notes of the scale.

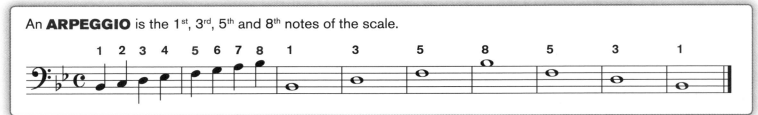

COUNTRY GARDENS—*Name the key. Before you play, notice how loud the crescendo becomes.*

English Folk Song

Allegro

163

CAMPTOWN RACES—*Before you play, notice how soft or loud each dynamic change becomes.*

Stephen Foster

Lively

164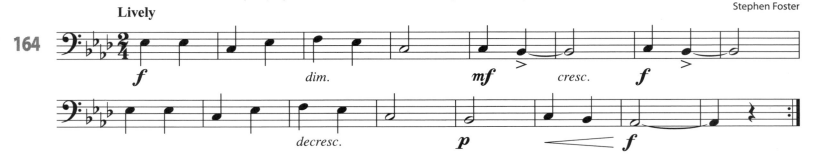

37

WHEN THE SAINTS GO MARCHING IN—*Full band arrangement.*

American Gospel Hymn

Austrian composer **Franz Joseph Haydn** (1732–1809) was one of the most important composers of the Classical period. He is best known for his many symphonies, string quartets, masses, and his oratorios *The Creation* and *The Seasons*.

SURPRISE SYMPHONY—*This piece includes a "surprise" created by dynamics. Can you find the big surprise? Discuss with your teacher the characteristics of music written during this period. Listen to the recording of this piece and describe those characteristics.*

Franz Joseph Haydn

HALF-STEP HASSLE—*Practice your chromatic skills.*

HILARIOUS HALF STEPS—*Here is another chromatic challenge. Name the notes before you play.*

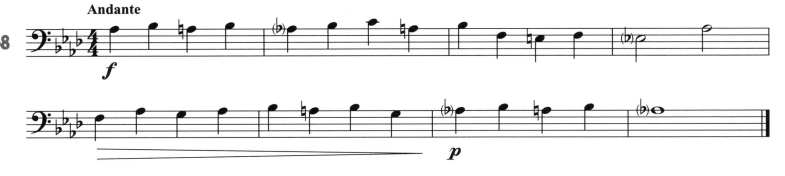

SYMPHONIC THEME FROM SYMPHONY NO. 1—*Is this a major or minor key?*

Gustav Mahler

169

An **ETUDE** is a "study" piece, or an exercise that helps you practice a specific technique.

ETUDE—*This exercise helps you become more comfortable with your chromatic notes.*

170

German composer and organist **Johann Sebastian Bach** (1685–1750) is considered to be one of the greatest composers of all time. He lived during the Baroque era and is best known for his cantatas, many works for organ, *Magnificat*, *St. John Passion* and *St. Matthew Passion*.

Modest Petrovich Mussorgsky (1839–1881) was a Russian composer who often used his country's history and folklore to inspire his compositions, such as *Boris Godunov*, *Night on Bald Mountain* and *Pictures at an Exhibition*, which includes *The Great Gate of Kiev*.

CHORALE—*Full band arrangement. Is this a major or minor key?*

Johann Sebastian Bach

171

A **RALLENTANDO** or **RITARDANDO** is an indication that the tempo is supposed to become gradually slower. It is indicated with the abbreviation *rall.* or *rit.*

THE GREAT GATE OF KIEV—*Full band arrangement.* Pictures at an Exhibition *represents a tour through an art gallery. In addition to form and color, music uses many of the same concepts as the visual arts.*

Modest Mussorgsky

172

▶ Complete the **SOUND CHECK** near the end of your book.

Level 6: Sound Performance

A **SOLO** is a piece that is performed alone or with accompaniment. Before playing this piece, watch and listen to it being performed on the DVD.

SOLO: SCARBOROUGH FAIR—*This solo has a piano accompaniment.*

Traditional English Ballad

Piano Accompaniment

174 THE BLUE-TAIL FLY (duet)—*Switch parts on the repeat.*

American Minstrel Song

> A **TRIO** is a composition in which three different parts are played by three performers at the same time.

> Many factors go into creating a great performance. Develop a list of things you think a performer should do to prepare for a performance. You might include such things as being on time, being prepared and practicing.

175 MOLLY MALONE (trio)—*Learn all three parts.*

Traditional Irish Ballad

TIME TRIALS—*Count and clap this exercise before you play. This piece reviews all the meters you have learned.*

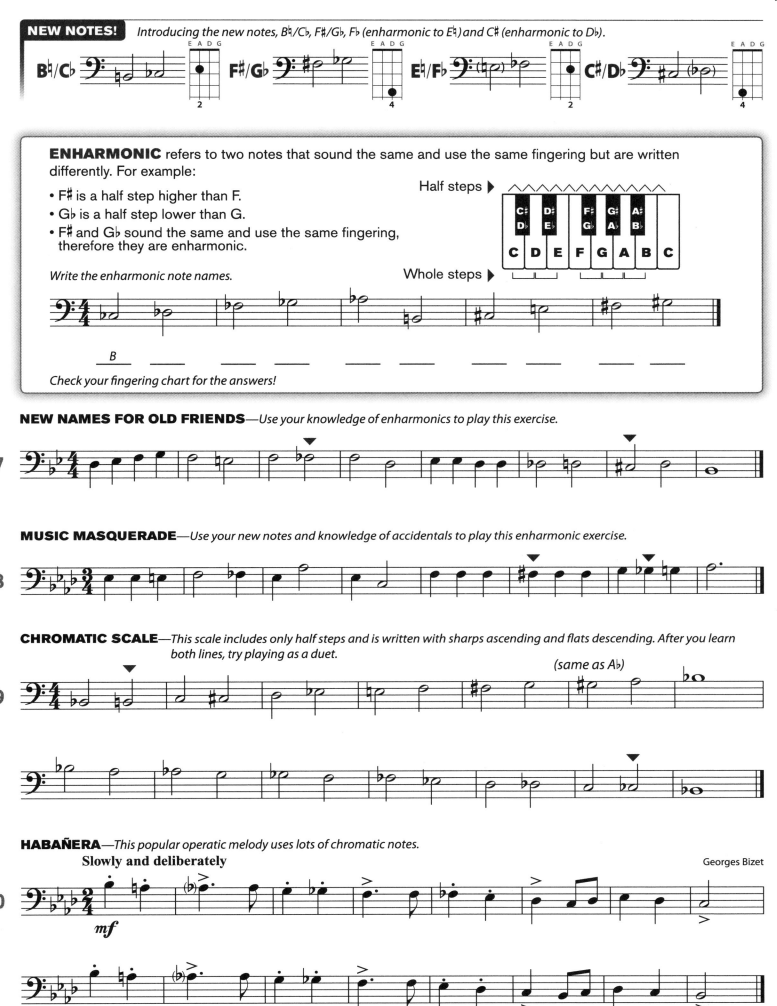

NEW NOTES! *Introducing the new notes, B♮/C♭, F♯/G♭, F♭ (enharmonic to E♮) and C♯ (enharmonic to D♭).*

ENHARMONIC refers to two notes that sound the same and use the same fingering but are written differently. For example:

- F♯ is a half step higher than F.
- G♭ is a half step lower than G.
- F♯ and G♭ sound the same and use the same fingering, therefore they are enharmonic.

Write the enharmonic note names.

Check your fingering chart for the answers!

NEW NAMES FOR OLD FRIENDS—*Use your knowledge of enharmonics to play this exercise.*

77

MUSIC MASQUERADE—*Use your new notes and knowledge of accidentals to play this enharmonic exercise.*

78

CHROMATIC SCALE—*This scale includes only half steps and is written with sharps ascending and flats descending. After you learn both lines, try playing as a duet.*

(same as A♭)

79

HABAÑERA—*This popular operatic melody uses lots of chromatic notes.*

Slowly and deliberately

Georges Bizet

80

mf

42

O CANADA—*This is the Canadian National Anthem. Play this in four-measure phrases by breathing after the long notes.*

Calixa Lavallée

GRANT US PEACE (round)—*Play this well-known round with the full band or as a trio.*

Traditional

TAKE A RIDE ON THE BLUES TRAIN—*Full band arrangement. Choose from the notes provided and make up a part as you play. This is called* **IMPROVISATION**. *Your director will indicate when it is your turn to improvise.*

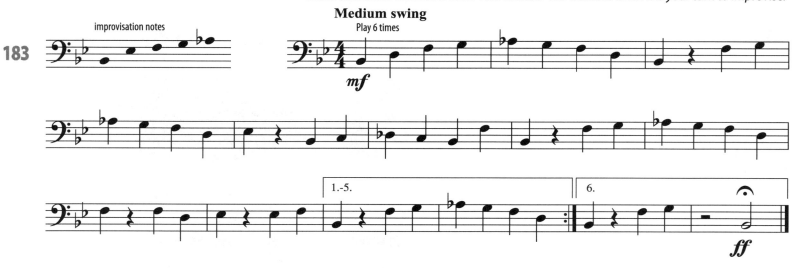

▶ Complete the **SOUND CHECK** near the end of your book.

Scales, Arpeggios, Warm-Up Chorales and Etudes*

Key of F Major

SCALE & ARPEGGIO

CHORALE IN CONCERT F MAJOR—*Full band arrangement.*

SCALE ETUDE

INTERVAL ETUDE

Key of B♭ Major

SCALE & ARPEGGIO

CHORALE IN CONCERT B♭ MAJOR—*Full band arrangement.*

SCALE ETUDE

INTERVAL ETUDE

*Scale and Etude exercises may be played with other instruments but are not always in unison.

44

Key of E♭ Major

SCALE & ARPEGGIO

192

CHORALE IN CONCERT E♭ MAJOR—*Full band arrangement.*

193

mf

SCALE ETUDE

194

INTERVAL ETUDE

195

Key of A♭ Major

SCALE & ARPEGGIO

196

CHORALE IN CONCERT A♭ MAJOR—*Full band arrangement.*

197

mf

SCALE ETUDE

198

INTERVAL ETUDE

199

Rhythm Studies

ETUDE #1

ETUDE #2

ETUDE #3

ETUDE #4

ETUDE #5

Sound Check

Level 1
Check off each skill you have mastered.

___ Posture

___ Instrument assembly

___ New rhythms

___ Hand position

___ New notes

___ Fermata

Level 2
Check off each skill you have mastered.

___ Conducting in $\frac{2}{4}$ and $\frac{4}{4}$ time

___ Playing p and f

___ New rhythms

___ New notes

Level 3
Check off each skill you have mastered.

___ Conducting in $\frac{3}{4}$ time

___ Repeats

___ Playing mp and mf

___ Accents

___ New notes

___ Pickup notes

Level 4
Check off each skill you have mastered.

___ Legato

___ Composing a piece of music

___ Identifying major and minor keys

___ Staccato

___ Understanding concert etiquette

___ D.C. al Fine

Level 5
Check off each skill you have mastered.

___ Playing a scale

___ Rallentando or ritardando

___ Playing in a variety of styles

___ Arpeggio

___ New notes

___ Crescendo and decrescendo (or diminuendo)

Level 6
Check off each skill you have mastered.

___ Playing a solo

___ Enharmonics

___ Improvisation

___ Playing ensembles

___ Chromatic scale

___ Playing rounds

Glossary

1st and 2nd endings – play the 1st ending the first time through; repeat the music, but skip over the 1st ending on the repeat and play the 2nd ending instead

accent (>) – play the note with a strong attack

accidentals (♯, ♭, ♮) – *see page 4*

alla marcia – play in the style of a march

allegro – a fast tempo

andante – a moderate walking tempo

arpeggio – the notes of a chord played one after another

articulation – indicates how a note should be played

bass clef – indicates the fourth line of the staff is F

chromatics – a series of notes that move in half steps

conductor – leads groups of musicians using specific hand and arm patterns

courtesy accidentals – help remind you of the key signature; occur after another accidental or recent key change; enclosed in parentheses

crescendo – gradually play louder

D.C. al Fine – repeat from the beginning and play to the *Fine*

D.S. al Fine – repeat from the sign (𝄋) and play to the *Fine*

decrescendo or diminuendo – gradually play softer

divisi – indicates where two notes appear at the same time

dot – increases the length of a note by half its value

double bar line – indicates the end of a section

duet – a composition for two performers

dynamics – change in volume

enharmonic – refers to two notes that sound the same and use the same fingering but are written differently

etude – a "study" piece, or an exercise that helps you practice a specific technique

fermata – hold a note or rest longer than its normal duration

Fine – the end of a piece of music

forte (f) – play loudly

harmony – two or more notes played at the same time

improvisation – creating music as you play

interlude – a short musical piece

interval – the distance between two notes

key signature – appears at the beginning of the staff, and indicates which notes will be played sharp or flat

largo – a slow tempo

ledger line – short, horizontal line used to extend the staff either higher or lower

legato (–) – an articulation or style of playing that is smooth and connected

mezzo forte (mf) – medium loud

mezzo piano (mp) – medium soft

moderato – a medium tempo

multiple-measure rest – indicates more than one full measure of rest; the number above the staff indicates how many measures to rest

octave – the interval of an 8th

one-measure repeat (𝄍) – play the previous measure again

phrase – a musical idea that ends with a breath

piano (p) – play softly

pickup note – occurs before the first complete measure of a phrase

rallentando – becoming gradually slower

rehearsal mark – reference number or letter in a box above the staff

repeat sign – go back to the beginning and play the piece again

right-facing repeat – indicates where to begin repeating the music

ritardando – becoming gradually slower

round – music in which players start the piece at different times, creating interesting harmonies and accompaniments

scale – a series of notes that ascend or descend stepwise within a key; the lowest and highest notes of the scale are always the same letter name and are an octave apart

solo – when one person is performing alone or with accompaniment

staccato (·) – an articulation or style of playing that is light and separated

style marking – sometimes used instead of a tempo marking to help musicians understand the feeling the composer would like the music to convey

syncopation – occurs when there is emphasis on a weak beat

tempo markings – indicate the speed of the music

theme and variation – a compositional technique in which the composer clearly states a melody (theme), then changes it by adding contrasting variations

tie – a curved line that connects two or more notes of the same pitch; the tied notes are played as one longer note with the combined value of both notes

time signature or meter – indicates the number of beats (counts) in each measure and the type of note that receives one beat

treble clef – indicates the second line of the staff is G

trio – a composition in which three different parts are played by three performers at the same time

tutti – everyone plays together

unison – two or more parts play the same note

waltz – a popular dance in $\frac{3}{4}$ time

Electric Bass Fingering Chart

○ = open string
❶ = index finger
❷ = middle finger
❸ = ring finger
❹ = little finger

1st fret

2nd fret

3rd fret

4th fret

5th fret

E A D G

E   F   F♯   G♭

G   G♯   A♭   A

A♯   B♭   B   C   C♯   D♭   D

D♯   E♭   E   F   F♯   G♭   G

G♯   A♭   A   A♯   B♭   B   C

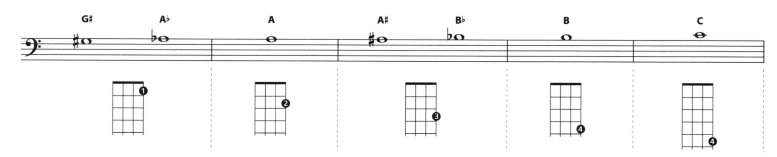